Zoom in on
MEDICAL ROBOTS

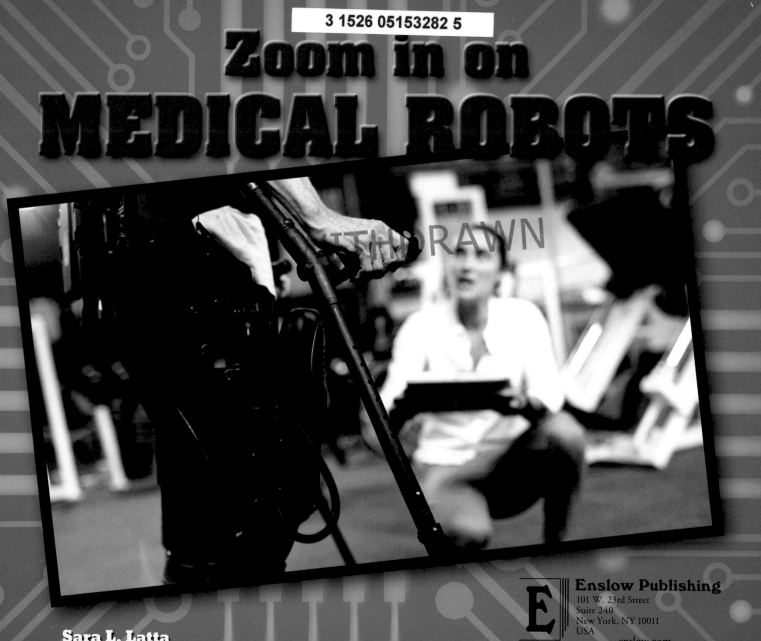

Sara L. Latta

E **Enslow Publishing**
101 W. 23rd Street
Suite 240
New York, NY 10011
USA

enslow.com

WORDS TO KNOW

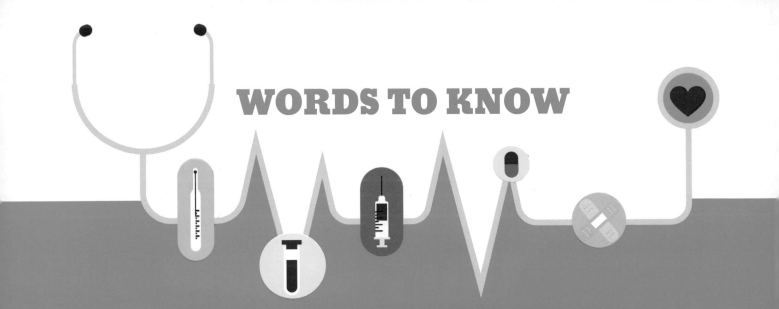

medical Having to do with medicine or the treatment of illness and injuries.

patient A person who is being treated for an illness or injury.

robot A programmable machine that can carry out a series of actions by itself.

sensor A robot part that detects light, temperature, pressure, sound, or motion.

stethoscope An instrument used for listening to someone's heart or breathing.

surgeon A doctor who can carry out operations (surgery).

thermometer An instrument used to measure temperature.

CONTENTS

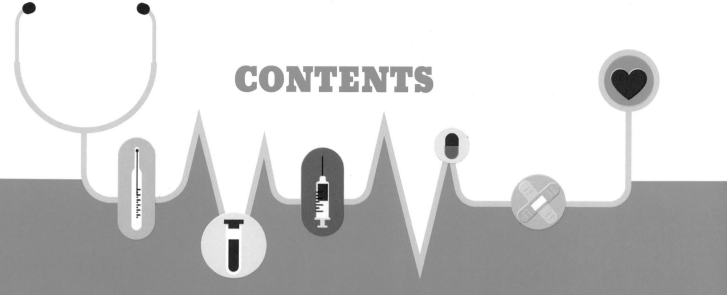

A boy and a nurse talk with Pepper, a robot that helps hospital visitors.

Medical Robots

Doctors and nurses help sick people get better. They use many machines and instruments. Thermometers tell them if a patient has a fever. Stethoscopes let them listen to the sound of the heart. *Lub-dub. Lub-dub.* Now, doctors and nurses have a new set of tools. They use robots.

Robots and computers can help doctors do surgery.

What Are Robots?

Robots are machines. They can do jobs by themselves. Computers control most robots. The computers tell the robots what to do. Robots have parts that allow the robot to move, grab, turn, or lift. They have sensors like cameras or microphones. The sensors tell the robot about what is nearby.

What's in a Name?

The word "robot" comes from a Czech word. It means "forced work."

What Do Medical Robots Look Like?

Medical robots come in many shapes and sizes. One hospital uses robots to deliver clean sheets and meals

PARO, a baby seal robot, is a good friend for this hospital patient.

to patients. The robots carry away dirty sheets and empty the trash. They are about four feet tall.

Another robot looks like a cute baby seal. Patients can hold it in their arms. It acts like a real pet. Sick people feel better when they cuddle with this robot.

Robots and Surgery

When people are sick or hurt, they may need an operation, or surgery. Doctors make openings in the body to take care of the problem. These doctors are called surgeons.

Hospital Help

In some hospitals, robots help surgeons do operations. The robots have four arms. Three arms carry tiny tools. The

Doctors and nurses use a robot to help them do surgery.

surgeon uses a computer to control the arms. A fourth arm carries a camera. The camera shows the surgeon what is happening on a computer screen. The camera makes the image inside the body look bigger.

The robots help the surgeons get into small places too large for their fingers. It is as though surgeons could shrink themselves and climb inside the body of their patients!

Doctors' Helpers

Robots help doctors make smaller openings in the body. Patients heal faster after the operation. They don't hurt as much.

This robot lets a doctor at one place visit with a patient at a different place.

Robots Help Surgeons Near and Far

It can be hard for some people to get to the kind of doctor who can do the operations they need. Soldiers may be hurt in a far-off country with few doctors skilled at operating. With robots helping, the doctor does not even have to be in the same room as the patient. In fact, doctors can operate on patients thousands of miles away. Doctors may someday use robots to operate on people in outer space.

Robots and People on the Move

Accidents or diseases leave some people unable to feel or move parts of their bodies. Some use wheelchairs to get around. They may need help to eat or drink. Robots can help these people do more things for themselves.

By wearing a special cap, a person can control a robot's arm with his brain.

Handy Helpers

People who can no longer use their arms can control a robot hand. They imagine picking up a candy bar with their own hand. Their brains send a signal to the robot. With practice, they can make the robot pick up the candy bar. The robot arm carries the candy bar to their mouth.

Brainwaves

Today, people can control robots with their brains only in the lab. In a few years, more people will get to do this in their everyday lives.

Walking with a Robot

Wheelchairs are a good way for many people to get around. But always sitting can be bad for the body. Robots help some people who cannot move their legs. They allow them to stand and walk.

These robots attach to the person's legs and hips. The robots move their legs and hips forward. People using this robot keep their balance by using crutches.

Robotic legs can help people walk.

Mighty Mini Robots

Not all robots are large. Imagine swallowing a pill filled with a huge number of robots. Each robot would be so small you could not see it with the naked eye. Such a pill does not exist yet. But scientists are building such tiny robots. They hope that doctors can soon use mini robots to treat sick people.

Computer artwork shows how a nanobot would inject a drug into a cancer (red) in a human body. The drug would kill the cancer cells.

Mini Robots at Work

Cancer can make people very sick. Cancer happens when cells in the body that are not normal divide and spread out of control. Doctors treat cancer with drugs. The drugs kill the cancer cells. They kill healthy cells, too. This can make a patient even sicker.

Scientists are building mini robots that can find and deliver drugs only to the cancer cells. The drugs would not kill the healthy cells. This would be a better way to treat people with cancer.

Mini Bots

Scientists have made mini robots with tiny motors. Stomach acids power the motors, like gas powers a car. Other scientists use magnets to steer robots around the body.

Muscle Power

Other tiny robots could roam the bloodstream. Muscle cells made in the lab power the little robot. They would look for signs of disease. These little robots have sensors that can "see" or "smell" their surroundings. If they find a problem, they send signals to doctors.

This tiny medical robot is less than one inch (two centimeters) long. It could stay inside the body to treat disease.

ACTIVITY:
MAKE A GRABBER

You have learned how robots can pick up and carry objects. Now it's time to make your own robot "hands."

What you'll need:

wire clothes hanger (the type with cardboard tube attached to the open-ended wire)
an adult helper
duct tape
PVC plastic pipe, 1 inch (2.5 centimeters) in diameter and at least 3 feet (1 meter) long
wooden dowel, ¼ inch (½ cm) in diameter and at least 3 feet (1 m) long

How to make it:

1. Take the cardboard tube off the hanger.
2. Bend the two open ends of the hanger toward each other to form the "hands" of the grabber.

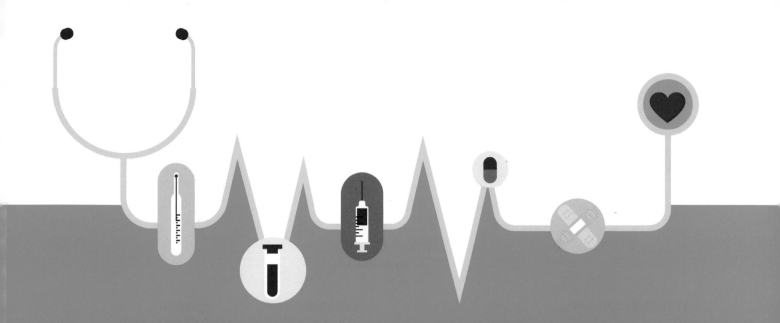

3. Ask an adult to straighten out the curved part of the hanger (the part that hangs from your closet rod).

4. Use duct tape to attach a wooden dowel to the straightened part of the hanger.

5. Place the dowel and straightened part of the hanger into one end of the PVC pipe. The "hands" of the hanger should poke out of the other end.

6. Wrap rubber bands or duct tape around each of the "hands."

7. Pull on the dowel to make the "hands" come together. Push on the dowel to pull them apart.

8. Try out your robot hands! What can you pick up with them?

LEARN MORE

Books

Schulman, Mark. *TIME for Kids Explorers: Robots.* New York, NY: TIME for Kids, 2014.

Stewart, Melissa. *National Geographic Readers: Robots.* Washington, DC: National Geographic Children's Books, 2014.

Tuchman, Gail. *Robots.* New York, NY: Scholastic, 2015.

Websites

Robotics: Facts
idahoptv.org/sciencetrek/topics/robots/facts.cfm
Check out many interesting facts about robots.

Robots for Kids
sciencekids.co.nz/robots.html
Check out the world of robots with games, facts, projects, quizzes, and videos.

INDEX

Published in 2018 by Enslow Publishing, LLC.
101 W. 23rd Street, Suite 240, New York, NY 10011

Copyright © 2018 by Enslow Publishing, LLC.
All rights reserved.

No part of this book may be reproduced by any means without the written permission of the publisher.

Library of Congress Cataloging-in-Publication Data

Names: Latta, Sara L., author.
Title: Zoom in on medical robots / Sara L. Latta.
Description: New York : Enslow Publishing, 2018. | Series: Zoom in on robots | Includes bibliographical references and index.
Identifiers: LCCN 2017018934| ISBN 9780766092280 (library bound book) | ISBN 9780766094383 (pbk.) | ISBN 9780766094390 (6 pack)
Subjects: LCSH: Robots—Juvenile literature. | Robotics—Juvenile literature. | Medical technology—Juvenile literature. | Medical innovations—Juvenile literature.
Classification: LCC TJ211.2 .L376 2018 | DDC 629.8/93—dc23
LC record available at https://lccn.loc.gov/2017018934

Printed in the United States of America

To Our Readers: We have done our best to make sure all website addresses in this book were active and appropriate when we went to press. However, the author and the publisher have no control over and assume no liability for the material available on those websites or on any websites they may link to. Any comments or suggestions can be sent by email to customerservice@enslow.com.

Photo Credits: Cover, p. 1 Caiaimage/Trevor Adeline/Getty Images; p. 4 John Thys/AFP/Getty Images; pp. 6, 10 Media for Medical/Universal Images Group/Getty Images; p. 8 Yamaguchi Haruyoshi/Corbis News/Getty Images; p. 12 The Boston Globe/Getty Images; p. 15 University of Minnesota; p. 17 Kathryn Scott Osler/The Denver Post/Getty Images; p. 19 Roger Harris/Science Source; p. 21 Yoshikazu Tsuno/AFP/Getty Images; graphic elements cover, p. 1 (background) Perzeus/Shutterstock.com, pp. 2, 3, 22, 23 Elena_Che/Shutterstock.com, pp. 5, 9, 14, 18, Vector Tradition/Shutterstock.com, pp. 16, 20 Artem Twin/Shutterstock.com.